T0143165

A Quick-Tip Pocket Guide

The Drama - Free Workweek

* * *

How to Manage Difficult People for
Workplace and Career Success

by Treivor Branch

ISBN: 978-1-4269-5433-7 (sc)
ISBN: 978-1-4269-5432-0 (e)

Trafford rev. 12/30/2011

 www.trafford.com

North America & international
toll-free: 1 888 232 4444 (USA & Canada)
phone: 250 383 6864 ♦ fax: 812 355 4082

This book is dedicated to all the hard-working women and men who have the unfortunate task of dealing with workplace drama and the difficult people who cause it.

Contents

Acknowledgements

Oh my, so many people to thank and so little space!
I am so grateful for my loving supporting family - my mom, sisters, brothers, nieces and nephews. Thank you for believing in me and understanding when I could not spend as much time with you as you may have liked during this project. Thank you all so much for your support and the space to stay focused.

Thank you to all my friends and clients for giving me such great insight into your workplace drama. Thank you for your support and your eagerness to read the book.

Thank you to the difficult people who have made this all possible. Without you, this book would never have been written. Thank you for the opportunity to learn and grow, to be better and do better. Thank you for helping me and others see how we should never be.

Introduction

*"The single most important ingredient
in the formula of success is knowing
how to get along with people."*
—Theodore Roosevelt

The United States Department of Labor's Bureau of Labor Statistics indicates that the 20-something year olds entering the workforce are likely to change jobs seven to ten times during the course of their careers. These job changes are often precipitated by such top factors as greater opportunity, greater compensation, and the search for decreased drama.

That's right, one of the top reasons people change jobs is to get away from drama in the workplace. The drama they are trying to flee is often brought on by difficult bosses and difficult co-workers. They are essentially in pursuit of the utopian workplace.

The awful truth is it does not exist. Difficult people show up in every workplace. Running from them does not make them go away. So what can you do?

You can learn how to manage them. Don't be dismayed, this does not mean you grin and bear it, letting the stress of working with difficult people build up until one day you explode. Instead, managing difficult people means identifying who they are and taking steps to lessen their impact on your career, your well-being and your life.

Outlined in the pages to follow are quick tips to manage workplace drama and the difficult people who cause it. You will even come to recognize if you may be the difficult person and what you can do to change your habits.

Note: All names in the scenarios listed, except those reported in public media outlets, have been changed to protect the innocent and not-so-innocent.

Managing
When You're
The Employee

Beware of
The Backstabber

Laurie was one of the first people who welcomed me when I started at the company. She introduced me to the team, showed me the ropes, and made me feel comfortable. It wasn't long before I considered her a friend and we began sharing bits and pieces about our personal lives. I soon realized this was a big mistake. One day I let Laurie know that I was considering a job offer I received from a competitor. Laurie apparently let this "slip", as she called it, into the ear of our boss who promptly let me know he didn't like "defectors". He began to limit my exposure to certain clients and projects. I was devastated! Laurie and I had been chums for eight long months; I would have never expected her to stab me in the back.

Who Is The Backstabber?

The Backstabber can be the person in the office who seems to be very helpful. However, that help can come at a price and one day The Backstabber will cash in. It is usually when you least expect it; when The Backstabber has gained your trust and you have divulged some intimate details that she can use against you.

What You Can Do

1. **Express Your Feelings**. It is important to approach The Backstabber and let her know what she did was wrong and unappreciated. Manage your emotions before approaching The Backstabber. Do not approach in anger, but in a manner of true concern about her trustworthiness and integrity. Let The Backstabber know what you shared with her was private and you trusted she would hold it in confidence. Let The Backstabber know how this affected your relationship with her and what that relationship will look like going forward.

2. **Be Friendly, Yet Cautious**. When you start a new job it is natural to make friends and align yourself with those from whom you can learn or who are willing to share. However, be careful what you share and how much you share, especially about your personal pursuits. Backstabbers look for any piece of information that can potentially be used against you when the time is right.

3. **Experience Is The Best Teacher.** Unfortunately, some backstabbers are so crafty that you don't recognize their true intentions until it is too late. Learn from this encounter and be careful what you share going forward.

4. **Don't Be Deterred.** Don't let The Backstabber deter you from building positive relationships within the workplace. Continue to share and learn from others within the organization. Build your network at every level throughout the organization and be engaging.

5. **Have Confidants Outside Of Work.** Utilize your network outside of work to share your personal pursuits. This network should be totally unrelated to those you work with. It should provide you with a great outlet to brainstorm ideas as well as vent your frustrations.

Glean From
The Gossiper – Or Not!

At first I was entertained by Megan's 'information'. I was able to catch up on the latest news in the office, and around the world, since she was always aware of current events. I knew some of her information could be considered gossip, but I didn't realize how serious this could be until I became one of her current events.

One day I was in the cafeteria when I overheard some of my co-workers whispering about something Megan had shared with them. One person even came over and said, "I'm so sorry to hear about your situation." I inquired what that was, and she shared with me that Megan was spreading news that I was getting a divorce and on the verge of a nervous breakdown! I was shocked! Yes, my husband and I are having some problems and I shared this with Megan in private once, but I didn't expect her to tell anyone! How did I allow this to happen? I can't stand to look at her now.

Who Is The Gossiper?

The Gossiper is generally someone who has a strong desire to be liked and included. The Gossiper feels that being an information source for all things juicy will give her the in she is looking for to build and maintain relationships. The Gossiper does not discriminate; she will gossip about management as well as the cleaning crew. She also knows no bounds. No topic is off limits. She will share what she has *heard* about who is getting promoted or fired to personal information about who is getting married or divorced.

What You Can Do

1. **Don't Be Smitten.** The Gossiper can be engaging and entertaining for a moment, especially if you have a job that is not very exciting. However, gossip is the spreading of rumors, real or imagined, and can negatively impact productivity and morale. Don't engage in malicious gossip and be careful what you share about yourself.

2. **Redirect The Conversation.** One of the most effective ways to deal with The Gossiper is to redirect the conversation by changing the subject. Don't be afraid to get a little rude and cut The Gossiper off in mid-sentence to redirect the conversation. You can say something like, *"Wait, I have to tell you what I was able to get done today...."*

3. **Walk Away.** You can choose which conversations you engage in or not. If The Gossiper approaches you with the latest and greatest workplace news, simply walk away. You can let her know, *"I'm very busy. I don't have time to chat with you."* After a few times of experiencing this response from you, The Gossiper will get the hint that you are not interested in what she has to say and she will limit her contact with you.

4. **Notify The Subject.** If The Gossiper has shared some information with you about a particular individual, bring it to the attention of the person being discussed. Let the person know you are sharing this with them out of concern so that they are aware of what is going on. In this way, the person is informed of what has occurred and can approach The Gossiper to nip it in the bud.

5. **Confront The Gossiper.** Do not hesitate to approach The Gossiper and let her know how her gossiping is affecting productivity and morale within the organization. Let her know that if she continues with this behavior, you will bring it to the attention of management or human resources due to its negative and malicious nature.

6. **Don't Spread Gossip.** Do not be quick to listen to The Gossiper and share in her exploits by spreading what you have heard. If The Gossiper shares something with you, keep it to yourself. If everyone does the same, the gossip will become a smoldering flame rather than a spreading wildfire.

5 Facts About Gossip

1. **Everyone gossips** – If you have ever shared any information about a person without their permission, positive or negative, real or imagined, you have engaged in gossiping. However, The Gossiper makes it a sport and an important aspect of their relationship development strategy.

2. **There are two types of gossip** – positive and negative.

3. **Negative gossip is malicious** and seeks to undermine or destroy the reputation of another. Negative gossip is a form of bullying.

4. **Positive gossip can be constructive** and boost the reputation of an employee, particularly in front of key decision-makers. For instance, sharing that someone is a great problem-solver or is a good golf player.

5. **Gossip cannot be completely eliminated**, but it can be controlled. Company policies can be put in place to control negative gossip and the spreading of rumors. However, it is the responsibility of each individual within the organization to control the gossip. Employees confronted with gossip can choose to change the subject, stop the gossiper as soon as they begin to gossip, or simply walk away from the conversation.

How The Backstabber Differs
from The Gossiper

The Backstabber	The Gossiper
1. Chief aim is to undermine and destroy the reputation of the subject.	1. Chief aim is to win friends and influence others.
2. Strategically shares the information with management or those in some position of authority or influence as it relates the subject.	2. Carefree in sharing information at the employee level. Less likely to share with management.
3. Is fully aware of what they are doing and the impact on the subject.	3. May think they are engaging in harmless conversation without consideration of the consequences and overall impact.

Don't Fall With
The Downer

Alice reminds me of the commercial with the motto 'I've fallen and I can't get up', except this is not a commercial and she has not physically fallen. She also does not have that nifty gadget around her neck to press for help. I'm the gadget since she runs to me every time she has 'fallen'. It is beginning to drain me emotionally. I don't want to hurt her feelings, but I can't be her shoulder to cry on anymore. It is bringing me down.

Who Is The Downer?

The Downer is good at playing the victim. This is the person who will make remarks such as, *"that's not fair."* She feels everyone in the workplace is against her. The Downer often seems overwhelmed and easily distracted. She seeks out every opportunity to complain to a listening ear. She complains about everything from the chair she is sitting on to the management at the company.

What You Can Do

1. **Don't Affirm.** The key to dealing with The Downer is to avoid affirming her feelings. Affirming the downer will only escalate the whining and you will be the one she runs to all the time.

2. **Don't Disagree**. Just as you don't affirm The Downer, don't disagree with her either. This will also escalate the whining as she tries to get you to affirm her.

3. **Don't Offer Solutions.** Don't try to solve the problem for her. The Downer does not want solutions. This will only escalate the situation as she becomes critical of your solutions, letting you know why they won't work until you affirm her as she originally intended.

4. **Cut It Short.** Don't let the Downer waste your valuable time. Give her a time limit as soon as she approaches you. Say something like, *"I only have two minutes, what's up?"* As soon as the two minutes are up, let her know you have to get back to work. Simply say, *"Sorry to hear that but I have quite a bit to get done."*

5. **Redirect The Downer**. Try redirecting the focus of the conversation to something positive. Ask the Downer, *"what is going right for you today?"* Depending upon what The Downer is whining about, it may be best to encourage her to speak with someone in the human resources department, especially if it is a matter of a serious nature.

The Mysterious
Dr. Jekyll and Mr. Hyde

I once saw a sign which described Bill perfectly. The sign read, "I can go from zero to psycho in 3.5 seconds." One moment he can be the nicest guy you ever met, very helpful and encouraging. Then without warning he is a totally different person, yelling, using profanity, turning red in the face and you are left wondering, where did this monster come from? Unfortunately, none of us in the office have been able to figure out what causes this sudden change in his personality.

Who Is Dr. Jekyll and Mr. Hyde?

Aside from the popular character featured in the book by Robert Louis Stevenson, the Dr. Jekyll and Mr. Hyde in the workplace is a mystery and often quite disturbing. It is unknown what may trigger a person to switch from Dr. Jekyll to Mr. Hyde. It could be something as simple as someone's facial expression when they greeted him or something someone said.

What You Can Do

1. **Alert Your Human Resources Department.** It is important to note that some people you work with may not be well psychologically. For this reason, any repeated uncontrolled outbursts must be brought to the attention of your human resources department. Your human resources department will know how to get to the root of the problem and ensure the person receives the appropriate help, such as referring the person to counselors through an Employee Assistance Program.

2. **Remain Calm.** Resist the urge to respond in an emotional manner. Don't scream or yell back at Dr. Jekyll and Mr. Hyde. Walk away and allow him time to calm down. If you must speak to him during the rant, keep your voice calm and even-toned when speaking to him.

3. **Listen.** Show your concern by listening to him. Listen to hear what the problem is. Do not approach while he is in the rage. Let him calm down and then ask what made him so angry. Ask him how you can support him.

4. **Reply With Understanding.** Acknowledge that it is good to get his feelings out. However, convince him to take a break to cool off, such as a walk outside or an early lunch.

Do Business With
The Dumper

During a coaching session one of my clients was able to discover that one of the biggest pangs of distress she was experiencing in her job was due to a dumper. She was consistently allowing a peer to dump his work on her. This was affecting her performance as well as her well-being. She was so busy doing his work she barely had time to catch up on her own. As a result, she was constantly stressed out because she was missing key deadlines and suffering from complete overwhelm.

Who Is The Dumper?

The Dumper is a person who consistently off-loads their work by dumping it on you or some other passive person in the office they know won't say no.

Dumpers look for those passive people in the office who won't push back when they dump on them. They call it delegation, but it is really dumping.

What You Can Do

1. **Identify The Behavior.** Recognize when someone is inappropriately dumping their workload. Know the signs of when someone is simply delegating in a pinch, or is a dumper. A dumper repeatedly off-loads their less desirable work onto you, often with little or no notice beforehand.

2. **Never Fear.** You may allow yourself to be dumped on for fear of being labeled as someone who is not a 'team-player'. However, which would you prefer; to be seen as someone who is not a team-player or, someone who can't get their job done? The latter will put you out of a job much faster than the former.

3. **Nip It In The Bud, Tactfully.** You can halt this disruptive behavior in a positive manner. The next time the dumper comes around simply say, *"I'd love to help you, but I'm swamped and have several deadlines I have to meet."*

   The dumper will get the hint and at the same time have no hard feelings because you didn't come off abrasive, you were honest, and you indicated your *willingness* to help out. At the same time, you communicated that you are at your limit.

4. **Lend A Hand, When You Can.** Do not hesitate to help out when you can; however, make sure your own work will not suffer.

5. **Get The Details**. Get the complete details about the job and what is expected of you. Make sure to ask about the deadline for the project as well as your piece of the project.

6. **Set Ground Rules.** Make it very clear to the individual requesting your assistance what you are able to assist with. Let them know how much time you can devote to the project without jeopardizing your other responsibilities. Make sure you are both clear on deadlines for the project. Also, let them know if something they are requesting is beyond your skill set so that they may look for assistance elsewhere.

Stop
The Swiper

"Swiper no swiping!" -Dora The Explorer

From this quote you can tell there are little ones in my home who adore Dora The Explorer. One of the characters on this popular children's cartoon is a sneaky fox named Swiper who steals anything he can get his paws on from Dora and her friends. This crafty character got me thinking about people in the workplace. Do you have a Swiper at work - that person who will steal not just your stapler, but also your ideas? Well, you're not alone. This type of person is one of the most common workplace offenders.

Who Is The Swiper?

The Swiper is often someone who lacks confidence in their own ideas. They are both intimidated by and envious of you so they seek to imitate you. Remember, imitation is the best form of flattery. However, The Swiper who steals your ideas can make work very frustrating and, hinder you from progressing because you might be afraid to present your best ideas. However, there is a way to beat the swiper at his own game.

What You Can Do

1. **Share Ideas Strategically.** Have a good idea? Share it with your team openly, not individual team members privately. In this way, all will know who the originator is and, this makes it hard for The Swiper to claim it as their own when the whole team heard it from your mouth first.

2. **Write It Out.** Send your ideas in an email or submit them in a formal dated proposal when reasonable. Putting it in writing creates a documented testimonial that you are the originator of the idea. This also makes it easy in the event you need to get your idea in front of key decision makers.

3. **Constructively Confront.** Constructive confrontation is always my favorite because it is so effective. Of course, you don't want to blurt out *"Swiper no swiping!"* like Dora and her friends. However, you can say, *"I notice you like my ideas and I'm flattered. Let's put our heads together to come up with some solid ideas we can present together."* In this way, you build a bridge while putting a stop to the swiping. The Swiper just may be too embarrassed by the confrontation to say no.

4. **Say Nothing and Keep It Moving.** Of course, you always have the option to say nothing. You don't *have* to confront The Swiper. Determine how much this affects

you. If you are able to brush it off, kudos to you; ignore it and keep it moving. It all depends on your level of comfort with this type of menacing behavior. Assess how it is affecting your career and your well-being.

Saying nothing is the best tactic if The Swiper is your boss. It is your job to make the boss look good. A good boss will remember how you stood by them and reward your loyalty.

Get To Know
The Know-It-All

Samantha is an Ivy League grad who believes that any graduate from any other school cannot possibly be as smart as she is. She walks around adding her two cents to projects which do not involve her and critiquing the work of every team member. I can't speak for our other co-workers, but I know it is driving me nuts! It has gotten to the point where I'm starting to second guess my own intelligence, although I graduated top of my class and have earned two promotions to get where I am.

Who Is The Know-It-All?

The Know-It-All is generally a very confident and competent individual who has no problem with assertiveness. Often a perfectionist who has a high need for control and is very outspoken.

What You Can Do

1. **Don't Take It Personally.** The Know-It-All is not necessarily trying to take a dig at you as much as she is trying to highlight her own ideas, however crass the method.

2. **Be Well Prepared.** When entering a meeting where a know-it-all is present, have all your facts as it relates to the idea you are putting forth. Be sure you don't skimp on the details.

3. **Don't Be Intimidated.** The Know-It-All has very little patience for ideas and views which she feels are inferior to her own so she may butt in while you are presenting your idea. Acknowledge her input, but continue putting forth your idea by using a statement such as, *"Thank you for your input, but as I was saying..."* or *"Please do not interrupt while I am speaking. You can present your thoughts once I have finished."*

4. **Beat Them To The Punch.** Welcome the thoughts and opinions of The Know-It-All. Solicit her input before she gets an opportunity to rudely butt in. Her opinions will eventually become less offensive and more constructive.

5. **Learn From The Know-It-All.** Take this opportunity to use her as a mentor and look for opportunities to collaborate so that both of your ideas are put forth in a mutually acceptable manner.

Disarm
The Dirty Joker

Mike started out likeable enough, but then he developed a penchant for making sarcastic remarks and not-so-kind jokes about my suggestions, especially during meetings or in front of others.

Who Is The Dirty Joker?

The Dirty Joker is often a minion of The Bully. He is a weasel who teases you in an effort to undermine your expertise; all in the name of 'fun'. A favorite remark of the dirty joker is *"come on, lighten up."* All the while knowing his true aim is to make you look like an idiot.

The Dirty Joker usually has one of the following hidden agendas: to win favor with a bully or know-it-all, to undermine your ideas in order to highlight his own or, he is a complete jerk who just likes to start trouble in the office (yes, they do exist).

What You Can Do

1. **Keep Your Cool.** The Dirty Joker is more of an annoyance than anything else. However, keep your cool; do not fall into victim mode and start whining or lash out in anger.

2. **Assertively Confront.** Confront The Dirty Joker as soon as you notice the behavior. Speak to him one-on-one in a private setting to find out what is fueling his behavior and let him know it is childish, disruptive and will not be tolerated.

3. **Ask Them To Elaborate**. Don't ever ask, *"why are you picking on me?"* You will only be setting yourself up for further humiliation. Instead, ask The Dirty Joker pointed questions such as, *"do you have a point you want to make?"* or *"what exactly are you trying to say?"*, or make a statement such as, *"please elaborate."*

Managing
The Micro-Manager

My boss is a control freak. She comes by my desk and stands over my shoulder while I'm typing and will make comments like, "why are doing that?" or "I would prefer if you did this…" One day she asked me where I was going during a break at a team meeting and when I said to the bathroom, she had the nerve to say, "OK two minutes" and hold up her fingers. It was a ten minute break. I could not believe it. Her micro-management is driving me crazy! I feel like I can't breathe without her breathing down my neck.

Who Is The Micro-Manager?

The Micro-Manager is a control freak with trust issues. While she has assembled a team of great performers, she does not trust that the work will be completed on time and to her standards. This attitude can stem from past experience with poor performers where she got burned due to their poor work quality. The Micro-Manager also believes that anything done right needs her input so she finds it difficult to loose control and allow her team members to work autonomously.

What You Can Do?

1. **Consult**. Consult with The Micro-Manager at the end of each workweek to prepare for the following week. This will help you both set expectations and help you understand what she would like you to focus on immediately in the upcoming week. This consultation will be an eye-opener and help you better manage your workweek to fulfill her needs.

2. **Be Proactive**. Remember, The Micro-Manager has issues with trust and control. Make her feel at ease by being proactive with keeping her in the loop. Send her regular updates on what you are working on and the progress of any projects. Bring issues to her attention as soon as they arise. Copy her on emails, as appropriate. Being proactive in this manner will help build her trust that you are on top of things. She will come to value your proactive approach to keeping her informed, thus lessening her need to manage your every move.

3. **Examine Yourself.** Perform a self-assessment of your performance. Have you done anything which would give The Micro-Manager any reason to doubt your ability to get the job done to her satisfaction? Have you ever been untrustworthy? Presented her with sloppy or inaccurate reports?

4. **Seek To Understand.** If none of the above apply to you, then have a discussion with The Micro-Manager. Your goal is to understand why she micro-manages you, so listening is key. Don't be quick to respond and do not become defensive. By simply listening and verifying what you hear you are more likely to unearth the reason

for her mistrust and be able to reach a mutual agreement on how you can work better together.

5. **Instill Confidence.** During the discussion with The Micro-Manager point to the quality of your work and past successes. Have documentation, if possible, which shows the high quality of your work and how it has benefited the team or made her shine. Let the Micro-Manager know you are fully competent and your goal is to support the team, not destroy it, so you will always give 110%.

6. **Share Your Feelings.** Do not get overly emotional, however, share with the Micro-Manager how her behavior makes you feel. Use statements such as *"When you do…I feel …."*

7. **Seek A Solution.** Ask The Micro-Manager what you need to do to gain her trust and allow you the space to work autonomously. The Micro-Manager will not change overnight, so suggest a trial period such as two weeks where she will not interfere with your work and micro-manage. At the end of the trial period, have a discussion to assess your work and her feelings. If all goes well, extend this period until eventually she is comfortable with allowing you to work independently.

Topple
The Steamroller

Mary is only 5 feet tall, but we call her 'The Steamroller'. The last thing you want to do is get on her bad side. She will flatten anyone who gets in her way. One day Charlie decided to challenge one of her suggestions at a team meeting. You could hear a pin drop when he made his statement because everyone knew what was coming next. Mary ripped his suggestion apart pointing out every flaw and not flinching as she took aim at his lack of research and preparation. It was so bad I almost saw him shed a tear.

Who Is The Steamroller?

The Steamroller is usually a haughty person with a big ego. Anyone who dares to challenge is quickly squashed and humiliated as an example to all the rest. The Steamroller loves to let you know they're the boss.

What You Can Do

1. **Manage Your Emotions.** Do not show fear or anger when dealing with The Steamroller. Be assertive, yet not aggressive. Seek to gain the respect of The Steamroller not the victory over her.

2. **Don't Put Them On The Spot.** Present your idea as a request for her input or assistance and, present it in private whenever possible. Use a statement such as, *"I'd like to get your thoughts on this..."* or present a question such as, *"Do you think it would be best if...."*

3. **Stick To The Facts**. When confronting The Steamroller or making a suggestion, present the facts, do not rely on your opinion. When presenting a new idea or opposing viewpoint, have supporting documentation which shows why your idea is sound. When The Steamroller comes back with a harsh remark or tone, follow with a comment such as, *"Let me share with you some facts"* or a question such as, *"What do you propose?"*

4. **Stand Your Ground.** Do not back down without a civil discussion. Engage in a constructive discussion around the matter. Listen for key concerns in her point of view. Always show respect for The Steamroller's position and authority. However, don't be afraid to agree to disagree.

Back Off
The Bully

It was my first job out of high school. I was finally entering the world of work. Excited, nervous and a little scared because I had great expectations, yet I did not know what to expect. As soon as I entered the office, I noticed something very strange; I was the youngest female and the only female minority. My first 6 months on the job were just as I'd imagined, I was being trained in various areas and enjoying my work. I was quiet, yet personable and kind to all of my co-workers. However, I was never invited out to lunch with the other women or made to feel included.

One of my bosses made it clear to me she did not like me very much. She was constantly making comments about some aspect of my demeanor, calling me "Ms. Goody Two-Shoes" or in some way embarrassing and humiliating me in front of others. It wasn't long before the other women joined in on the humiliation and I realized my boss had become the leader of a workplace gang, as I called it. I was eventually put through several more years of what can only be described as a nightmare. I came out of the situation so stressed that I was hospitalized with a life-altering illness only weeks after quitting my job there.

At the time I was going through this situation, I did not know what I was experiencing was called bullying, but I knew it was wrong. I went from being a chipper happy new employee to being sick to my stomach with the thought of going into work each day. I felt I had nowhere to turn. I felt everyone was against me and the situation seemed hopeless. There was a time when the head of my department came out of his office screaming at me in front of everyone, particularly after I had filed a complaint with our internal Equal Employment Opportunity department. Unfortunately, at the time, I thought my complaint would somehow remain anonymous. How foolish I was back then. As the head of my department screamed at me in front of the entire office, the rest of the women chuckled as I was being reprimanded for filing a hostile environment complaint.

I went home many days crying and not understanding why this was happening to me. I now know that what I experienced was bullying. I now know that the emotional and physical ailments I experienced at such a young age while working there were the result of the bullying. I have come to experience the message of the Bible which states, whatever is meant for evil God will turn to good. I have been blessed with the wonderful opportunity to share what I have learned throughout my career. I now help others who are being bullied by educating them on how to stand up for themselves in the workplace and the necessary steps to take in such situations.

Who Is The Bully?

The Bully is the most harmful and disruptive person to have in the workplace. The Bully is someone who has low self-esteem and a high level of insecurity. The bully thrives on making others, usually a weaker victim or someone by whom they are intimidated, feel just as bad as or worse than they do.

What You Can Do

1. **Take A Break.** Bullying is one of the top stressors in the workplace and can cause severe stress-related health problems. In view of this, it is essential for anyone being bullied at work to first take a stress break. This includes utilizing paid sick leave or personal time off to distance yourself from the situation, visit a mental health provider as well as your medical practitioner. Often, stress related health problems have very little warning signs until it is too late.

2. **Document.** If you have not done so already, document the instances of bullying. Your documentation should include the names of all bullies, dates of occurrences, and detailed descriptions of the bullying; include both subtle and blatant instances of bullying. Also, include the names of any witnesses to the bullying incidents. Further, record what attempts (if any) were made on your behalf to address or stop the bullying when it occurred as well as the results of such interventions. This information is helpful for the next step, as well as good information to bring to the attention of an attorney for review.

3. **Constructively Confront.** Meet with the bully to address the situation. During this discussion it is important to effectively manage your emotions. Be clear about what has occurred and how it makes you feel, however, do not get explosive, yell, or in any way provoke or give in to a hostile exchange. Listen as much as you speak and seek a resolution to the situation. Ask open-ended questions such as, *"How can we work better together?"* Share with the bully what your expectations are going forward. Be prepared for a negative response; bullies typically do not like to be confronted and there may be some negative

feedback. However, do not let this deter you from taking this important step.

4. **Report.** Make your human resources department (HR) aware of the situation; particularly if the bullying continues or worsens following your confrontation. Be sure to present your documentation. In addition, consult an attorney, as some instances of bullying may violate discrimination policies and be eligible for legal action.

5. **Plan Your Exit.** Although you have followed the steps above, it is important to note that because bullying is not an illegal form of harassment some employers ignore the problem. In view of this, there is the chance that your employer will do nothing to alleviate the bullying situation. In addition, your attempts to transfer to another department may be blocked by the bully, particularly if the bully is your boss. For reasons such as this, it is important to develop an exit strategy as soon as you notice you have become the target of a bully.

Have a plan B and be prepared to resign your position. In addition, be prepared to be laid off, as also occurs in situations where an individual is being bullied at work. You can be proactive in addressing these issues by having a current resume which you begin circulating when you notice there is a problem. Note, I do not recommend this for every instance in which you come across a difficult person. However, when you are the target of a bully, especially if the bully is the boss, which is usually the case, the chances of resolution occurring in the current position are not likely. For your well-being and your career, it is best to leave the situation rather than stay.

A Few Stats on Bullying In the United States

A 2010 survey conducted by the Workplace Bullying Institute (workplacebullying.org) and Zogby International (zogby.com) revealed the following:

- 35% of the U.S. workforce has experienced bullying (an estimated 53.5 million Americans)

- 15% of workers report being a bystander witnessing bullying in the workplace

- 62% of bullies are men

- 58% of those targeted by bullies are women

- 80% of cases involve women bullying other women

- 68% of bullying involves same-gender harassment

For more information download the full survey at: http://www.workplacebullying.org/research/WBI-NatlSurvey2010.html

Source: Workplace Bullying Institute© 2010

How The Bully Differs From The Steamroller

To be clear, the tactics of The Steamroller are a form of bullying. However, there are a few traits which make The Steamroller someone you are more likely to effectively manage and eventually form a positive relationship with than The Bully.

The Bully	The Steamroller
1. Seeks out victims.	1. Only attacks those who get in their way.
2. Chief aim is to psychologically torment and derail the career of weaker victims.	2. Chief aim is to stop the challenger from getting in their way.
3. Not open to reason; they only want to make your life a nightmare.	3. Open to reason when an opposing point of view is presented in a non-challenging manner.
4. Has low self-esteem and is intimidated by those they perceive as smarter or in some way 'better' than they are.	4. Has high self-esteem and a huge ego. Detests those they perceive as less intelligent.

5. Enjoys the company of brown-nosers and kiss-ups.	5. Respects those who do not easily cower when they bark. ***Note of caution***: If The Steamroller is approached in the wrong manner, they can become The Bully with you as the target.

Managing When You're The Boss

Take The Lead

"A leader is one who knows the way, goes the way, and shows the way."
— John Maxwell

It is important for managers, supervisors, and team leaders to lead by example. Employees are more confident and productive when they see and hear from their leaders on a regular basis. Taking the lead to maximize relationships contributes to the success of your team and your organization.

Policies Rule

"Peace and friendship with all mankind is our wisest policy,
and I wish we may be permitted to pursue it."
-Thomas Jefferson

Don't skimp on policies. One of the best ways to manage difficult behaviors in the workplace is to institute a respectful workplace policy which includes actions to be taken against those who create a climate of incivility and disrespect. The policy should cover actions such as lying, gossiping, bullying, and other forms of disrespect.

For assistance with creating a respectful workplace policy, visit www.thebranchsolution.com for a free consultation.

Get Rid of Toxins

"Civility costs nothing, and buys everything."
-Mary Wortley Montagu

Don't tolerate toxic behavior. When you become privy to employees exhibiting toxic behavior in your workplace, have a discussion to find out why they are exhibiting such behavior. Reprimand them verbally; warning them of the consequences if such behavior continues. If the behavior continues, put it in writing and outline clearly what the consequences will be for such behavior including termination.

Do not hesitate to terminate employees who make the workplace undesirable for others. Why lose several good employees because of one bad apple. Make sure you have all supporting documentation of their offensive behavior and any ways in which they have violated company policy prior to terminating.

Spy Not

"Leaders must be close enough to relate to others, but far enough ahead to motivate them."
- John Maxwell

Don't ask employees to spy on one another. Such tactics foster an environment of distrust, destroys morale, and creates negative competition.

Instead, be proactive in building relationships with your employees. Show genuine interest in them on a personal level, not just as an employee. Let them know they can come to you when they have concerns or need to talk. Make sure your *open door policy* includes an open door.

Give Feedback

"One of the true tests of leadership is the ability to recognize a problem before it becomes an emergency."
-Arnold H. Glasgow

You are the person who keeps your team motivated and inspired. Uplift and encourage with constructive feedback on a regular basis. Don't wait until formal feedback processes. Spend time walking around your department, observing, and giving positive feedback. If your team is dispersed in various locations, pick up the phone.

If an employee's performance is lacking, have a discussion with them in private as soon as you notice there is a problem. Give them a chance to turn it around well before the formal review process. Offer to support them in any way you reasonably can.

Set The Tone

"Conflict is inevitable, but combat is optional."
-Max Lucado

Set the tone for effective conflict management and confronting difficult situations. Don't erupt at your employees over trivial mistakes or disagreements. Remain even-tempered and don't let your emotions get the better of you. Constructively resolve conflicts by focusing on the problem, not the person. Discuss issues in private if they involve only one or two employees.

Share Much Share Often

"If you want to build a ship, don't drum up people together to collect wood and don't assign them tasks and work, but rather teach them to long for the endless immensity of the sea."
-Antoine de Saint-Exupery

Share with your team. Share your vision, your goals, hopes and dreams for the department. Ask for their feedback and solicit their suggestions on how the team can best achieve the goals. Assign tasks which fit with each individual's strengths.

When issues arise which may disrupt productivity or fuel the rumor mill, get ahead of it all by communicating early as much detail as possible about the situation.

Show Your Pride

"If your actions inspire others to dream more, learn more, do more and become more, you are a leader."
- John Quincy Adams

Show pride in your team. Be confident that you have picked a group of winners that have what it takes to succeed. Be careful not to micro-manage. Believe in them. Remind them of their strengths and why you chose them to be a part of the team.

If someone's work does not meet your standards. Assess whether they are in the right role. Afford them appropriate training or reassign them if necessary.

Managing
YOU

It All Starts With You

Whether you consider a person difficult or not has a lot to do with your personality and your attitude. A person you may perceive as difficult and hard to work with may be the easiest person to deal with for your co-worker.

For instance, if you have a hard time taking direction or accepting constructive criticism, you may find a micro-manager extremely difficult to deal with. On the other hand, your co-worker who craves direction, attention, and desires constant feedback may value the guidance of the micro-manager. Your co-worker will learn to use the instruction given by the micro-manager to their advantage.

The next time you are confronted with a difficult person, ask yourself the following:

1. Why do I perceive this person as difficult?

2. What is this experience highlighting about my personality?

3. What can I learn from this experience?

"I Don't Like That Man,
I Must Get To Know Him
Better"

I was reminded of this famous quote by Abraham Lincoln during a morning cartoon session with the children. It is amazing how quickly children can build bridges even after their initial interaction with one another may have been rocky. Unfortunately, somewhere along the line, some of us lose this quality as adults. However, it is a simple and profound concept. Some of the best friendships can come from getting to know the person whom you most dislike. As another great quote says, "Friendship is born at that moment when one person says to another, 'What! You too? I thought I was the only one" - C.S. Lewis.

By getting to know the person whom you dislike, you get to understand what makes them tick. You may even find the common ground that helps you understand why they are the way they are. For instance, if you dislike them because they have a hard as nails personality, you may find that they were hurt or stabbed in the back at one point, therefore, they have a guard up to protect themselves. You can then work from that informational point and find common ground because most people have been hurt at least once in their lives, whether in a professional or personal relationship.

By going beneath the surface to discover the person behind the tough exterior, you may find that the person is actually the complete opposite of what they pretend to be. However, you'll never know until you make the decision to *"get to know him better."*

A quick way to start is by inviting the person to lunch. For instance, on a Friday you can simply say, *"you look like you've had a tough week, let's take a break and grab a bite, my treat."* Who would turn down such a generous offer!

Develop Your Listening Skills

"To listen well is as powerful a means of communication and influence as to talk well."
-John Marshall

The most important step toward eliminating the drama in your relationship with a difficult person is to engage them in a private discussion. During this discussion you want to listen carefully to what is being said and what is not being said.

To be an effective listener, you need to listen without interrupting. If you hear something that displeases you, let the person finish their thought. When they are finished, verify what you heard by stating, *"What I heard was…is this what you meant?"* Validate their feelings or perceptions by acknowledging they may differ from your own. You may state, *"I understand you are feeling…..now, how can I support you?"*

Listening effectively and validating the feelings of the other person will increase your ability to reach a solution to the problem.

Don't Fight Fire
With Fire

"You don't have to attend every argument you're invited to."
—Author Unknown

When you are confronted by a difficult person, whatever you do, don't get emotionally hooked. You can't fight fire with fire. If a person is yelling at you or the situation is emotionally charged, the best thing you can do is end the confrontation by walking away. Revisit the issue at another time. A simple statement in a calm voice may be, *"I see emotions are running high right now. Let's take time to calm down and revisit this when we can hear each other out in a civilized manner."*

Avoid The Fight
To Be Right

"Without accepting the other person's thinking, you cannot further your own interest. You need the other's help to get results."
-Harri Holkeri

When managing a situation with a difficult person, avoid the fight to be right. The best relationships are often built on compromise not the win-lose. Sometimes you have to be willing to meet somewhere in the middle when dealing with others. If you insist it's your way or the highway, you will alienate those around you and become viewed as the difficult person.

Don't Get Sidetracked

"Hard work spotlights the character of people: some turn up their sleeves, some turn up their noses, and some don't turn up at all."
-Sam Ewing

Recognize that everyone does not have the same work ethic. Just because you show up everyday and give 110% does not mean all of your co-workers will do the same. It is important to understand this fact so that you do not become discouraged and develop the negative habits of the slackers in the office. Focusing on their lack of commitment will only make you resentful and ultimately result in you becoming a difficult person.

Don't Turn Anger into Danger

"Anger is only one letter short of danger."
-Author Unknown

When I saw this quote, it immediately made me think of how appropriate it is for the wannabe Steven Slaters in the workplace. Steven Slater is a JetBlue Flight Attendant who had 28 years of service when he snapped. Kudos to him for sticking it out for so long - Not. His actions on August 9, 2010 when he cursed out a passenger over the plane's public address system, grabbed a couple of beers, then opened the emergency slide hatch and slid away, showed he had been on the job with unresolved issues way too long.

Stunts like this don't just surface with the advent of an unruly passenger; they build up over time and culminate into explosive outbursts, tantrums, and dangerous reactions. The sigh of relief in Slater's incident is that the whole shenanigan took place on the ground instead of in the air. However, that does not excuse the danger of the situation and the trauma it may have caused some passengers; especially those with a fear of flying or children on the flight.

Slater is being hailed a hero by some and has garnered such a strong fan base that he is being considered for a reality TV show along with other lucrative offers. However, this situation highlights the real and present dangers that lurk inside the workplace when the emotional and mental well-being of employees is not properly addressed both by the employers and the employees.

As an employee, here are steps you can take before you become the next Steven Slater:

1. **Take Breaks.** These breaks include power naps during the day, if possible, lunch breaks away from the office, as well as using ALL of your vacation time and personal days.

2. **Speak Up.** When you are feeling overwhelmed, discriminated against, bullied or burned out; don't just vent to family members, friends, and co-workers, go to your company's human resources department. If you get no help there, seek outside counsel; in some cases your unaddressed concerns may be grounds for a lawsuit.

3. **Be Proactive.** Don't wait until it is too late. Be proactive in engaging professional help through your employer's Employee Assistance Program (EAP) or an outside counselor who specializes in workplace-stress-related matters.

4. **Have A Life Outside Of Work.** When not at work engage in things you enjoy such as spending time with family and friends, pursuing a hobby, or exercising to stay healthy and ease the stress of the workweek.

5. **Make A Change.** There are times in your career, when you will outgrow your current position. When you have been in the same job doing the same thing

for too long, the job can become mundane and you can become frustrated. Know when it is time for a change and make one. Yes, there is a recession, but don't let this stop you from circulating your resume because that is what you will eventually end up doing if you have an outburst and are fired. The best way to begin making a change is to start your job search internally. Keep your eyes and ears open and work your network to find out about new opportunities, then get a move on.

These are just a few steps I hope you will implement to manage your well-being at work before it is too late. Don't let workplace drama build up and put you and those around you in danger.

References

Fed-Up Flight Attendant Makes Sliding Exit, Newman, A., Rivera, R., The New York Times, August 9, 2010 http://www.nytimes.com/2010/08/10/nyregion/10attendant.html

JetBlue Guy Steven Slater: Hollywood's most wanted, Weiner, A., The Hollywood Reporter, October 14, 2010 http://www.hollywoodreporter.com/news/jetblue-guy-steven-slater-hollywoods-26734

12 Steps to Effectively Manage Conflict

Conflict is a natural part of human relations. In fact, conflict can serve as a catalyst for creativity and relationship development. However, it must be managed correctly; in a manner that will not provoke escalation. Do not view the management of the conflict as a win-lose situation. The ultimate goal is a win-win, whereby both parties can reach a mutually acceptable agreement regarding their relationship and interactions going forward. Here are 12 steps to get you started:

1. Forgive

   Take a listen to this free Forgiveness audio to learn why this step is so important: http://www.thedramafreeworkweek.com/search/label/Forgiveness

2. Determine that you want to resolve the conflict

3. Manage your emotions

4. Approach the individual in private

5. Listen

6. Verify what you have heard

7. Validate the concerns of the other person

8. Express your feelings

9. Focus on the problem, not the person

10. Be open to compromise

11. Keep talking until you reach a mutually acceptable agreement

12. Put it in writing

About The Author

Treivor Branch, Founder & CEO of The Branch Solution LLC, is a savvy Workplace Issues Consultant, Conflict Management Specialist, and Executive Career Coach who specializes in maximizing workplace relationships.

Ms. Branch is dedicated to helping career professionals overcome barriers to career success, managers become better leaders, and companies build positive productive work environments. Ms. Branch is located in Connecticut and brings to her practice over 20 years of corporate experience including over 12 years of experience in human resources management. She has proven skills in diagnosing workplace and career problems, identifying solutions, and bringing about positive change.

For more information about Ms. Branch and to receive her workplace success tips, visit The Branch Solution online at www.thebranchsolution.com.

Learn about more difficult people and schedule a Drama-Free Workweek Retreat for your managers and employees by visiting www.thedramafreeworkweek.com.